INSPIRED

LESSONS FROM LIVES WELL LIVED

INSPIRED

LESSONS FROM LIVES WELL LIVED

Tuakah E. Whiangar

VILLAGE TALES PUBLISHING
MINNEAPOLIS, MINNESOTA

© 2021 Tuakah E. Whiangar

All rights reserved. Copying, printing and distribution of this book without permission is a theft of the author's intellectual property. No part of this book may be reproduced, or transmitted in any form of electronic or mechanical, including photocopying, recording, or by any information storage and retrieval system without written permission from the publisher, except for the inclusion of brief quotation in a review.

A catalog record for this book is available from the Library of Congress:
Library of Congress Control Number: 2021907519
ISBN: 9781945408700
eISBN: 9781945408717

Published By:
Village Tales Publishing
Minneapolis, MN 55429

Layout and Cover Design by: OASS
Backcover photo by: Tehmen Whiangar
www.villagetalespublishing.com
www.oass.villagetalespublishing.com

Printed in the United States of America

DEDICATION

This book is dedicated to all the students of the JAKE MEMORIAL BAPTIST COLLEGE located in Monrovia, Liberia, and all those who love the Word of God, making much of it in their own lives and the lives of others.

Contents

INTRODUCTION 9
EXTRA-BIBLICAL EXAMPLES 10
Dr. Kwame Nkrumah 11
Dr. William R. Tolbert, Jr 14
Nelson Mandela 16
Dr. Martin Luther King, Jr. 18
Dr. Arikana Chihombari Quao 20
Missionaries to Liberia 22
BIBLICAL EXAMPLES OF INSPIRATION 25
Abraham 26
Jabez 28
King Jehoshaphat 33
Timothy 35
Three Hebrew Men (Daniel 3) 37
Noah (Genesis 6-9) 40
Job 43
Daniel 46
The Apostle Paul 48
SPECIAL EXAMPLE OF INSPIRATION 53
Inspired By God Himself 54
CONCLUSION 57
NOTES 58
BIBLIOGRAPHY 59

INTRODUCTION

God the Creator made us as social beings. He made us to live with other people and to socialize with them. As we live in proximity to other people, we learn from them, and they learn from us. Our gifts and unique talents benefit them as theirs benefit us.

The focus of this lesson is Inspiration. Inspiration is a two-way street: others inspire us as we inspire others. We are inspired by others simply by how they live their lives. In the same way, unknown to us, we inspire others by just how we live our life. By inspiration, we mean how a person's life affects the lives of others to respond positively in life.

We are going to consider three sources of inspiration in this study. First, we will give examples of people outside of the Bible who may have inspired others. Then, we shall consider characters from the Holy Bible who inspired others. The last source of inspiration is from God Himself.

PART ONE

EXTRA-BIBLICAL EXAMPLES

The history of man is full of examples of people who inspired others. Some of them are dead, and some are still alive. Some of the names that we are going to use are very familiar because they were renowned world leaders. The majority of them are Africans. Of the examples I have chosen, only a few of them are still alive. They were ordinary people just like us today.

Dr. Kwame Nkrumah

Many years ago, one of the Old Testament prophets spoke these words under the inspiration of the Spirit of God: *"The heart is deceitful above all things, and desperately wicked; who can know it?"*[1] We all can agree with the statement. The heart of man is deceitful and wicked because man is sinful and has a depraved nature.

Because of the condition of man's heart, we can get an understanding as to why people have been so wicked down through the years. One of the deceptions of the human heart is the belief that some human beings are better than other human beings. Some even go to the extent that some people on Earth are less human. Due to this deception, they believe that these so-called "less humans" can be treated in any way and do not even deserve to live.

It was this belief that carried people from Europe to Africa to do all that they did there. With no respect or regard for the Africans, their lands were forcibly taken away. Many were killed. If that was not enough, they colonized them and sold many into slavery. The records are there to prove that these things were done on the continent of Africa.

As time went on and the children of Africa began to get an education, they discovered the evils against them and their ancestors. This discovery inspired some of them to put their lives on the line by demanding freedom and independence from their colonial masters.

---

[1] Jeremiah 17:9

One of such men was the late Dr. Kwame Nkrumah. He was a Ghanaian, educated in the United States and Great Britain. He was one of the first activists to demand independence from British rule. Dr. Nkrumah cared less about what could happen to him, because as for him, it was time for someone to speak up for what was right, regardless of the consequences.

Because of his conviction and passion for his country and people, the colonizers granted Ghana its independence in 1957. Dr. Nkrumah was the first president of the country. Ghana became the first nation in colonial Africa to gain its independence from a European power.

Following that milestone event, Dr. Nkrumah was not satisfied. He wanted more to be done. His vision of freedom went beyond his country of birth. He wanted all of Africa to be freed. His famous statement was that *"Ghana's independence was meaningless if it was not linked with the total liberation of all of Africa."* Dr. Nkrumah's ultimate goal for Africa was a borderless continent, united, and speaking with one voice on the world scene.

In 1963, the heads of States in Africa met in Addis Ababa, Ethiopia, to decide on the future of the continent. Unfortunately, the delegates to this all-important conference were divided. The majority wanted a United Africa, but not right away. The other group wanted it NOW. Since that time, the topic for a United Africa keeps coming up in the Continent's semi-annual conference of Heads of States.

In recent times, Kwame Nkrumah's vision in the 1950s for a united Africa is still alive and well. Considering the global hatred, disrespect, and oppression of people of African descent, it is becoming more and more necessary for Africans to unite and speak with one voice.

Two contemporary personalities who have revived the "United Africa" vision are Kenyan Professor PLO Lumumba and Dr. Arikana Chihombori Quao. Through their speeches and vision for Africa, many today are inspired to think positively about Africa and the African heritage.

Dr. William R. Tolbert, Jr

Dr. Tolbert was the Vice President during the presidency of William V. S. Tubman in Liberia, West Africa. He served as Vice President for 20 years (1951-1971). Following the death of President Tubman, Dr. Tolbert became the president of Liberia. He served in that capacity from 1971 to 1980, when he was assassinated in a coup.

While he was vice president, Dr. Tolbert served as a good second-man. He was a good observer. He observed everything that was going on in the country and in the government. From his keen observation, when he became president, he began to correct some of the wrongs of the past. He began to do that by his example. The first action he took was going to work on time. Those who failed to follow his example were fired from their job. He later changed Liberia's time system from LIBERIAN STANDARD TIME to Universal Time to correspond with the time system in other neighboring African countries.

Dr. Tolbert was a visionary. He practiced what he preached. When he became president of Liberia, in his first speech, he assured the people of the country that he would transform Liberia into a country just like any other in the developed world.

It was during his administration that certain parts of the capital city were laid out. He built low-cost housing units and schools around the country in areas where there were no schools. He got involved in business and encouraged the people to get involved in agriculture.

Some of the people did not see the value of the president until after he was killed. It was then that they began to realize that he meant well for the country. How did he inspire others? His inspiration came from his practical examples. By his example, he proved that indeed, something "good" could come out of a country like Liberia. He empathized with the people. He saw their condition and identified with them. He did something to change the living condition of the people. *"From Mat to Mattress"* was his vision for ordinary people. The people's interests and needs were his interest and main focus. Liberia needs more leaders like the late Dr. William R. Tolbert, Jr.

Nelson Mandela

History is very important. It is crucial for a nation and a group of people. Throughout history, the people are informed about where they have been, obstacles they have encountered, and progress they have made. It helps them to know what to do in the present and how to face the future.

It is just now that some Africans are revisiting the history of the African continent and its people. It is just now that some Africans are beginning to understand what outsiders have done on the continent and its people's inhumane treatment.

Nelson Mandela was born and raised in South Africa. Before his time, people from Portugal, the Netherlands, and Great Britain went to South Africa searching for greener pastures. They met the Africans there. They cared less about who they were. Their lands were taken from them, and some of them were killed.

In 1910, the Union of South Africa was established. It was a mainly white union, excluding people of color. Around this time, the African National Congress was founded (1912) to protest the exclusion of black people from power.

In 1948, the pro-Afrikaner National Party came to power, with an emphasis on apartheid. Their goal was to put together a more rigorous and authoritarian rule than the previous segregationist policies in South Africa. While the white minority was cementing its power to segregate and suppress the black people, black opposition to this kind of behavior grew. One of the leaders of this opposition was Nelson Mandela.

He and others strongly opposed the system of apartheid that marginalized and excluded blacks and other people of color in the political and economic control within the country.

Because of Mandela's stand against the white minority government, he was arrested and put in jail for 27 unbroken years. While he was in that solitary confinement, Nelson was pressured to denounce his beliefs and turn away from his anti-government position. But he refused. As time went on, and that which was happening in South Africa finally came to the attention of the United Nations, some concessions were made. Under the leadership of F.W. De Klerk, the government of South Africa began to repeal apartheid laws that were against black people. That process set in motion a transition that eventually brought Nelson Mandela to power. President De Klerk freed him from jail.

Today, the name Nelson Mandela is a household name around the world. He was a man who stood up for that which was right. He was willing to pay any price to correct the wrong. He succeeded. Many of his colleagues did not live to see the end of the struggle against white minority rule in South Africa. People are inspired by Nelson's conviction and his determination to overthrow a wicked racist system.

Dr. Martin Luther King, Jr.

Dr. King was born on January 15, 1929, in Atlanta, Georgia, USA. At birth, he was called Michael King. Later, his father changed his name to Martin Luther King, in honor of the renowned German Theologian called Martin Luther. His father, who was also called Michael King, changed his name as well. That is how Dr. King came to be known as Martin Luther King, Jr.

At the time of his birth, racial segregation and Jim Crow Laws were at their highest peak in the United States. Racial segregation and Jim Crow Laws divided the people of the United States in two distinct groups: Black and White. Black people were freed from slavery after the Civil War, but they were not free citizens like white people. They were not even considered as "full citizens." They were not allowed to vote, and there were certain places they could not go or be.

The laws of the land made it difficult for them to have a good education, good jobs, or suitable housing. They were hated, disrespected, and oppressed by the white-dominated system. For some white people, they thought that the black people would remain as slaves indefinitely. They did not believe that black people are entitled to a good life and good treatment as white people. Therefore, when the blacks were freed from slavery, it made them so mad. Since they could no longer legally enslave anyone in the continental United States, they decided to enslave them socially, economically, and politically.

As Martin Luther King Jr grew older, he became aware of the social evil he and his people found themselves. He was not happy about it. Therefore, he decided to do something to change the racial injustice in his country. While he was in college, he wrote a letter to the editor of a newspaper in his city. In that letter, he demanded that Black people are entitled to the basic rights and opportunities as American citizens. This was the beginning of the movement that would later be known as the *"Civil Rights Movement."*

This movement challenged segregational laws that oppressed Black people. Through the struggles of the Movement, Black people were allowed finally to vote, sit anywhere on a city bus, and have access to facilities and places they were once not allowed. It was the efforts of Dr. Martin Luther King, Jr. and others, that gave freedom to many Black people in the United States. A Black person can now have access to any hotel or eat in any restaurant around the country because of them. Black people should be grateful to Dr. King and the "Movement" he started. He sacrificed his comfort and life for the sake of others.

Dr. King has not only inspired Black people, but people of all races. To have the courage and conviction to stand up for what is right is not easy. But God is always on the side of those who seek to do the right thing in life.

Dr. Arikana Chihombari Quao

Dr. Arikana Chihombari Quao was born in Zimbabwe, East Africa. During colonial time, the country was known as Rhodesia. Zimbabwe was colonized by the British. When the British arrived, the territory was Zambesia in 1896. The colonizers changed the name to Rhodesia, named in honor of Cecil Rhodes. The entire region was split into two parts: Northern Rhodesia and Southern Rhodesia. The Northern region became known as Zambia, and the South became known as Zimbabwe.

The colonizers committed many atrocities against the Africans. These atrocities were scantily documented and rarely discussed. The colonizers justified the atrocities because they felt that Africans were inferior beings and thus subject to extreme inhumane treatment.

Some of the atrocities were committed during the period known as the *"British Loot Law"* in Zimbabwe. The country was mapped up into regions based on the soil's fertility and the amount of rainfall. Region One had the best rainfall and the best soil. Region Two was close to Region One in terms of the quality of the soil. Region Three had insufficient rain and poor soil that was only good for cattle. Region Four had no rain. The soil was sandy and infested with things that made it inhabitable.

Following World War I & 2, British veterans were rewarded with almost 3000 acres of land in Zimbabwe. When those men arrived, Regions One and Two were given to them. Whoever they met there (the local Africans) were driven off their own land.

Dr. Arikana, who is from Zimbabwe, heard about these inhumane treatments carried out against her people. When she traveled to the United States to study, she spent many years there. She became a medical doctor and practiced medicine in the State of Tennessee for twenty-five years. Later, during her adult life, wherever she went, she observed that Africans are hated and disrespected all over the world. It is as though there is a universal agreement among the other races of people that Africans should be overlooked and disrespected.

She had always wondered about this and expressed her dissatisfaction that something should be done to address this behavior and change it. Then as God would have it, she was appointed by the African Union to serve as its special ambassador to the United States and the Americas.

This appointment gave Dr. Arikana the platform to address the mistreatments that had been carried out against people of African descent on the African continent, and outside of the continent. During this time, she had the opportunity to educate the people of Africa on these issues. Her goal has not only been to raise awareness but also to point out a path that may lead to more respect for Africa's people. The urgent call is for Africa to unite and speak with one voice on the world stage. The unity of Africa is not just for the Africans on the continent, but unity among all peoples of African descent scattered around the globe. The time in which we live has made this call urgent and very necessary. Many people are responding to this call. Dr. Arikana has not only inspired Africans on the continent, but people of African descent around the world.

Missionaries to Liberia

Liberians may disagree on the role that American missionaries played in inspiring others for good in Liberia. The missionaries came from different Mission Agencies in the United States. Our focus is on those who came from the Mid-Baptist Mission Organization, based in Cleveland, Ohio. These were the missionaries who started independent Baptist churches in Liberia. They started churches in Montserrado, Margibi, Grand Bassa, Rivercess, Nimba, and Bong Counties. In Liberia, these missionaries were known as Mid-Baptist missionaries. Many Christians in Liberia are familiar with these missionaries because they were saved in churches they started.

The missionaries started their church-planting ministry in the early 1930s. In those days, Africa was viewed by the outside world as the *"Dark Continent."* That label paints a negative picture of the continent and its people. Darkness suggests the absence of light. This "light" could not be physical light because the sun and the moon shine in Africa just as they do in other parts of the world. That being the case, the *"Dark Continent"* in the minds of those who gave this label could only refer to intellectual, social, and economic darkness. In other words, those who described the continent in those terms saw nothing of significance on the continent. The continent was perceived as being infested with all the negative things one can think of: disease, poisonous snakes, internal conflicts, etc. These people saw the place as a place of a death trap.

Yet, it was to this *"Dark Continent"* that the colonizers and missionaries, who were white, came. Each group had its own agenda. As for the missionaries, as far as we know, they came to give us the "Good News" of Jesus Christ. Some of them may have had other motives; we do not know and don't really care to know.

When the missionaries arrived, most of Liberia was not developed. Some feel that, for the most part, it is still not much developed. The missionaries who went into the interior parts of the country had much to contend with. The roads were terrible, and much of the basic necessities they had in America were absent. There was no electricity and running water in their homes. No showers. No flush toilets.

Literally, these people were pioneers. They were trailblazers. They had to start from scratch in order to make life in the new environment. They had to take baths in buckets, use pit toilets, and get water from the nearest creek. It was under such conditions they lived with their children for the sake of spreading the "Good News" of Jesus Christ.

Many Liberian Christians have not stopped to think about the sacrifices that some of those people had to make. What impresses me the most is that these people were total strangers doing these things for us.

How many Liberians have gone out of their way to make similar sacrifices for their fellow Liberians who are black like them? When Liberians leave the primitive life in the interior, many do not want to look back. Some of them who were able to travel to the United States or other developed countries worldwide seldom ever look back. Their home is now too primitive for them. Some even think that the place is too hot for them.

What the missionaries did should challenge all of us. If strangers were willing to sacrifice much to help our people, we should not do less. We should be inspired to follow their good examples to reach our own people with the "Good News" of salvation through Jesus Christ.

We can easily identify with these examples. They were people just like us. Nkrumah and Tolbert were leaders on the continent of Africa. Arikana, who is still alive, is also an African. Even though Dr. Martin Luther King, Jr is an American, his root can be traced to the continent of Africa. They all made a difference in their generation. We can follow their good examples to inspire others.

PART TWO

BIBLICAL EXAMPLES OF INSPIRATION

In this portion of the lesson, we shall look at some biblical characters. The focus is to discover how their lives inspired others and how we can draw inspiration from the way they lived and their decisions.

Abraham

What inspiration can we draw from this man? He was one of the heroes of the faith. He was one of the pioneers of the faith. What does it mean to be a pioneer? The dictionary gives us two meanings. 1) A pioneer is a person who is one of the first to settle in an area; 2) A pioneer is a person who begins or helps develop something new and prepares the way for others to follow.

The second definition suits the purpose of our study. Those who were pioneers in the faith were the first people to exercise trust in the true living God. They had none others before them. The positive decisions they made in their relationship with God set the tone for others to follow. People like Job, Daniel and his friends, and many others in the Bible fall in this group. Abraham was one of them.

When God called him, Abraham was probably not a believer in the true living God. Perhaps he was like many people during his days—idol worshippers. But when God called him, he listened and followed.

The Lord asked Abraham to do two difficult things. The first was for him to leave the land of his birth, to go to a land that God would show him. According to the story, Abraham did not question or argue with God. Instead, he quietly obeyed and immediately put his obedience into action. The second difficult request was for Abraham to offer his son, Isaac, as a sacrifice. Prior to this time, God had never asked anyone else to do such a thing. Therefore, Abraham had no one before him from whom to draw inspiration to make the right decision. He was a pioneer.

The Book of Hebrews tells us that Abraham did not hesitate to do what God asked him to do.[2] This was so because he believed God. He knew that God had the power to bring Isaac back to life.

Besides these difficult requests, God made some key promises to Abraham. The promise was three-fold: the promise of a seed, land, and that he would be the father of many nations. Regarding these promises, Abraham believed God, and it was credited to him as righteousness.[3]

What inspiration can we draw from the life of Abraham? We must believe God's word and act upon it.

---

2 Hebrews 11:17-19
3 Genesis 15:6

Jabez

Jabez's story is found in I Chronicles 4:9-10. Please permit me to share how I discover the story of Jabez in the Holy Bible. I did not hear it from any preacher. In the early 1980's when I was in college at the Temple Baptist Theological Seminary, located in Chattanooga, Tennessee, I came upon the story of Jabez. The course was Old Testament Survey. The assignment was to read through the Old Testament during the semester.

The immediate response was that it was an impossible assignment. But because I wanted to pass the course, I forced myself to make the impossible possible. Yes, indeed, it was possible. It was while I was reading through the Old Testament that I came upon the story of Jabez. For those of you who have never read through the Old Testament, I encourage you to try it. It will be a rewarding exercise. You will discover things that you never thought were in the Bible.

I Chronicles 4:9-10 reveals three things about Jabez. They are his reputation, his name, and what he did. Regarding his reputation, people viewed him as being more honorable than his brothers. This means that he was worthy of honor, a man of distinction. A similar thing was said about the believers in the city of Berea during the time of the Apostle Paul.[4] They were described as being "more noble." We discover from the text that they were described as such because of what they

---

4 Acts 17:11

did. Their response to the Word of God was one of open-mindedness, eagerness, and keen interest to learn.

Jabez was described as being honorable because of what he did. He did something that perhaps none of his brothers did not do. He identified his concerns and took them to God for help. What were those concerns? He asked for four things. Someone has said that his requests can be expressed or simplified by four words: grace, growth, security, and protection.

He asked God to bless him; this is grace. He wanted the unmerited favor of God upon his life. All the blessings of life come from God, the Creator. *"Every good gift and perfect gift, is from above, and cometh down from the Father of lights, with whom is no variableness, neither shadow of turning."*[5] When God blesses us, that blessing is an expression of His grace upon us. No one deserves it. No one can merit it. This is why God's blessings upon us should humble us. We should not be puffed up or proud because we have what others do not have. It was based on this fact that the Apostle Paul rebuked the Corinthian believers. *"For who sees anything different in you? What do you have that you did not receive? If then you received it, why do you boast as if you did not receive it?"*[6]

Jabez wanted God to bless him. This initial request was a summary of everything else he asked for. Naturally, we think of blessings in the form of money and material possessions. But that's not it all. God's blessings may also include good health, long life, and our spiritual well-being. All of this is by God's grace. The second thing that Jabez asked for was that God might enlarge his coast or his border. This suggests growth. The young man wanted growth in his life. He want-

---

5 James 1:17
6 I Corinthians 4:7

ed his territory and possessions to expand. He did not want stagnation. Sometimes we see stagnation in a country. Nothing tangible and exciting seems to be happening. Year after year, there seems to be no significant sign of development anywhere. When this happens in a nation, it brings despair, discouragement, depression, and the people's lack of inspiration. Jabez did not want any of this. He wanted growth that would bring hope and inspiration.

His third request was that God Himself may be with him in all of his undertakings. What a noble request! Jabez wanted God's presence in his life. He wanted God Himself to be a part of his life. This would provide security for him and guidance on the right path regarding his spiritual life.

Jabez's fourth and final request was for nothing else but protection. He asked the Lord to keep him from evil so that it may not grieve him. The word "evil" here speaks of calamity. Calamity is defined as an event causing significant and often sudden damage or distress; a disaster. It is marked by great loss and lasting distress, and mental anguish. Calamity can grieve us and be the cause of pain (whether physical or emotional). Jabez did not want any of this to be a part of his life and the lives of those related to him. We are told that God listened to him and granted him his requests.

There was a good reason for Jabez's four-fold requests. It had to do with his name. Jabez means, *"he will cause pain; sorrowful."* Perhaps he was given this name because of what his mother experienced during his birth and the subsequent sorrow that followed. He was not personally responsible for the negative effect his birth may have brought. It was one of those things that he had no control over. He did not want to be known as one who causes pain and brings sorrow. He wanted to change his story. It was this desire that drove him to the God of Israel, the one who alone could change his story.

Jabez was an Israelite. The nation of Israel was divided into twelve tribes. These tribes traced their roots to Jacob's twelve sons, whose name was changed to Israel by God. Two of the tribes may be described as "standing tall" above the rest in importance. They were the Tribe of Levi and the Tribe of Judah. Levi was the tribe set aside by God for priestly service. It was from this tribe that priests and the High Priest were taken. No one in Israel could be a priest or high priest who was not from the Tribe of Levi.

On the other hand, Judah was important because it was through this tribe that the Messiah came. According to I Chronicles 4, Jabez was from the Tribe of Judah. In this chapter, we find the family record or genealogy of the Tribe of Judah. It is in the midst of that record that we find the story of Jabez.

As an Israelite, Jabez was well informed about the God of Israel. Through oral tradition, he was probably informed about who this God was and the great things He had done for the nation of Israel. He was the God of Abraham, Isaac, and Jacob. It was He who delivered the Israelites from the bondage in Egypt. He caused them to walk on dry ground through the Great Sea. The God of Israel is the Almighty and the Creator of all things. Jabez, like all true believers in Israel, was convinced that their God could do the impossible. This strong belief motivated the young man to take his concerns to the God of Israel.

I personally have been inspired by the story of Jabez. There are certain things in life that we have no control over. None of us decided in which country to be born or in which family to be born. We had no control over which race to be born and how we would look physically.

But there are certain things that we have control over. We have control over our decisions based on the possibilities before us and what we can do to change our story. There is a God who has invited us to bring our burdens to Him.[7] It does not matter what the nature of the burden may be. God can handle them all.

It was from this realization that I began to pray for my country-Liberia. There are many negative things associated with this country. Because of these things, some Liberians have given up on the country in despair. As far as they are concerned, Liberia cannot be rescued from the direction it is heading. In other words, nothing good can come out of Liberia. But from Jabez's story, I discovered that there is hope and that hope is in God. He has the power to change Liberia's story as He did for Jabez. He alone is the way maker. I shall continue to pray for Liberia in particular and mother Africa in general. The Lord has already begun to answer my prayer. I invite you to join me in this endeavor.

---

7 Psalm 55:22

King Jehoshaphat

(II Chronicles 17:1-21:1; I Kings 22)

He was the son of King Asa, who was king of Judah. At this time, the Kingdom was divided. The Northern Kingdom was called Israel. Its capital city was Samaria. The Southern Kingdom was known as Judah. Its capital city was Jerusalem.

King Jehoshaphat did something that no other king did in Judah or Israel. He had great respect for the Word of God. He demonstrated this by consciously and deliberately making much of God's Word in his own life and the lives of others. He decided to expose his people to the Word of God. He selected leaders from his government, and along with the Levites and priests, sent them all over Judah, teaching the Word of God from city to city.

The result of the king's action was remarkable. The Lord was pleased with what he did. We are told that the fear of the Lord fell upon all the kingdoms of the land that were around Judah, such that they made no war with King Jehoshaphat. Also, the countries that had been Judah's enemies presented gifts to the King. He became powerful, and much development was carried out in Judah during his administration.

One inspiration from this King has to do with what he did with the Word of God; he made much of it in his own life and also in the lives of his people. The Word of God contains great and wonderful truths. Those who know these truths and have been blessed by them should share them with other people. This principle is in line with other parts of the

Scripture. *"Freely you have received, freely give."*[8] *"Go into all the world and preach the gospel to every creature."*[9] *"When a man's ways please the Lord, He makes even his enemies be at peace with him."*[10]

---

8 Matthew 10:8
9 Mark 16:15
10 Proverbs 16:17

Timothy

One of the New Testament books was named after this incredible young man. He grew up to be a great leader in the Bible. He was from the city of Lystra. During Paul's first missionary journey, he stopped in Lystra and Derbe and preached the gospel there. It is believed that it was at this time that Timothy heard the gospel of Jesus Christ and believed. The seed of God's Word had been planted in his heart through his mother and grandmother.

Following his conversion, the young man distinguished himself as a genuine believer in Jesus Christ. His life changed, and he committed himself to the work of the Lord. The people in Lystra, Derbe, and Iconium noticed the dramatic change in the life of Timothy. When the Apostle Paul and his missionary team returned in Lystra and Derbe, the believers in those cities highly recommended Timothy. They said many good things about him. This may have impressed Paul, which prompted him to recruit Timothy to be part of his missionary team.

The Apostle never regretted that decision. Timothy proved himself to be a faithful servant. He became one of Paul's trustworthy and dependable assistants. He was like the "number two" man to Paul. He was committed to the work of the gospel. His primary focus was to help in whatever way he could to ensure that God's work succeeds. His primary concern was not for position or to take the "number one" spot. He was not in a hurry to be promoted. This is a good quality for a true leader. At the appointed time, Timothy was elevated in his leadership role.

One important lesson we can learn from Timothy is the patience to wait to be promoted. Whatever position we occupy, we should seek to do our very best there, blossoming where we have been planted. With that attitude, jealousy, envy, and impatience can be avoided.

Three Hebrew Men (Daniel 3)

One of the most dramatic and interesting stories in the Bible has to do with three young Hebrew men. Their story is found in Daniel 3. They were called Hananiah, Mishael, and Azariah. The King of Babylon changed their names while they were in captivity. He called them Shadrach, Meshach, and Abednego.

These young men, along with their friend, who was called Daniel, had an unshakable faith in their God. Even though they were taken away from their home in Judah and carried to a foreign land, they did not forget their God.

They were men of conviction. Their conviction was based on the truth of God's Word. Shadrach, Meshach, and Abednego believed with all their hearts that there are right and wrong in life. According to God's instruction, it is wrong to worship any other gods besides the Holy Bible's God. This truth cannot be compromised or negotiated. It was unthinkable for them to consciously and deliberately do anything contrary to the absolute truth.

While in Babylon, these men faced tests that challenged their conviction. The first test had to do with the food in the new land. The people of Babylon did not know the true living God. They worshipped false gods.

Daniel and his three friends refused to eat the food that was given to them. Even though the story does not provide a reason for their decision, it could be that perhaps the menu contained some of the food they were forbidden to eat, according to Jewish laws. They requested a meal that was not questionable, that did not go against their dietary conviction.

Before the test or temptation came, the men already had their minds made up about what is wrong and what is right. Therefore, without hesitation, they chose to do the right thing. If we are not convinced about what is right and what is wrong, we will not know how to respond when temptation comes.

The second test had to do with Nebuchadnezzar's golden image. The King commanded that his people should bow down to his golden image and worship it. Anyone who refuses to do so would face the King's wrath. When the signals were given for all the people to bow down in unison and worship the golden image, Shadrach, Meshack, and Abednego refused to obey.

Quickly, someone reported them to the King. When the King investigated the allegation, it was found to be true. The King was furious. He felt insulted and belittled. His countenance changed. The King decided to teach the rebels a lesson. They were not going to get away with their challenge. Therefore, he commanded the fire to be heated seven times hotter than its actual temperature.

Shadrach, Meshach, and Abednego were not intimidated. They believed in their God. They were resolved to obey Him, no matter what the consequence would be. They were convinced that their God was able to deliver them from the burning fire. But if He chose not to do so, it was not going to change their decision. Their conviction positioned them to make the ultimate sacrifice to obey God.

What inspiration can we get from these men? We should follow their good example to be willing to make any sacrifice to do God's will. In a sense, they were pioneers in the exercise of their faith. They had no one before them from whom to draw inspiration as to what to do in the face of such a test. I am often reminded of the challenge in the Book of Hebrews regarding our struggle with sin. It says that none of us has struggled against sin unto blood. In other words, nobody has shed blood while struggling against sin. If Meshach, Shadrach, and Abednego were willing to go that far to obey God, how far should we be willing to go?

Noah (Genesis 6-9)

Noah is one of the well-known characters in the Old Testament. He became a prominent man in his time. His fame also extended beyond his time because of his faith in the true living God.

We do not know exactly the number of years that elapsed from the time of Adam up to Noah. But one thing is clear: people had become very wicked. The effect of Adam's sin was displayed everywhere. The Biblical narrative reveals that ". . . God saw that the wickedness of man was great in the Earth and that every imagination of the thoughts of his heart was only evil continually."[11] That was the spiritual condition of the people in Noah's day.

God decided to do something. Because of His holiness and justice, He chose to judge sin and those involved in it. He revealed His plan to Noah, who was different from all the other people. Noah feared God. His fear kept him from doing things that did not please God. This is what the Book of Hebrews has to say about Noah:

"By faith Noah, being warned of God of things not seen as yet, moved with fear, prepared an ark to the saving of his house; by the which he condemned the world, and became heir of the righteousness which is by faith."[12]

We discover from the story of Noah that he was a just man. He was blameless in his generation and walked with

---

[11] Genesis 6:5
[12] Hebrews 11:7

God. Noah knew God and had faith in Him. His faith was demonstrated by the way he lived his life. God rewarded him by revealing His plan to him. He was warned of what was to happen in his world. Noah believed God and took the warning seriously. He did exactly what God told him to do in order to escape the judgment that was to come.

God, in His mercy, always gives warning before bringing judgment. He warned Cain, but he never listened. The people in Sodom and Gomorrah received a warning through Lot, but they didn't take the warning seriously. Lot's wife was warned, but she did not obey.

Because Noah listened to God's warning and obeyed, he and his family did not have to regret anything. The people who drowned in the great flood must have regretted it as the floodwater began to cover the Earth. They failed to listen to Noah's warnings. They failed to take advantage of the three warnings from Noah. One of the warnings was Noah's preaching. I am quite sure he told the people what God had planned to do. This is confirmed by the fact that Noah was a preacher of righteousness. The second warning was the building of the ark, a huge structure. The seriousness and sincerity with which Noah went about to do such a thing he had never done before should have sent a message to the people. But they didn't get it. The third warning had to do with the animals. Of their own accord, they went to Noah into the ark, male and female. This alone should have rung a bell in the mind of the people. It was not normal. The people failed to see God's hand in the whole thing. They rebelled and remained in their unbelief.

The story of Noah is a warning for us today. The Bible tells us that God is going to bring another judgment in the future. It is going to be global just as it was in Noah's day. The difference is that this future judgment is going to be fire instead of water. The warning is found in the second epistle of Peter.[13] Just as God provided a way of escape during the first judgment, He has also offered a way of escape from the judgment to come. That way of escape is through His Son, Jesus Christ. Jesus tasted death on the cross to provide a way of escape for mankind. God has promised that all those who will believe in His Son will not perish but shall have everlasting life.[14]

There are some lessons we can learn from the story of Noah. The first lesson is that it is possible to be different in a culture where everyone seems to be going in the wrong direction. Noah lived a different life because of his fear of the Almighty God. A second lesson from this story is that God's judgment is not based on majority rule. It is based on His truth and justice. Because most people are for that which is wrong, it will not affect God's judgment. We see that happening in the world today. The majority's opinion seems to matter more today than what God had said. There seems to be no fear of God at all today.

---

13 II Peter 3
14 John 3:14-17

Job

Another Old Testament character who has inspired so many people was the man known as Job. He lived in the land of Uz. The exact location of Uz is uncertain. From the text, we discover that it had many pastures and crops (1:3) and that it was near a wilderness area (1:19). The land of Uz must have been close to the Sabeans and the Chaldeans to be raided (1:14-17). According to Matthew Henry, the area was in the Eastern part of Arabia, which lays towards Chaldea, near the Euphrates, probably not far from Ur of the Chaldees.[15]

Job was described as a blameless, upright man, feared God and avoided evil.[16] He was a rich man. He was blessed with ten children and had much possessions. He had many servants working for him.

Even though Job was a Godly man and tried to do what was right, he was not exempt from the uncertainties of life. However, the things that happened to Job were allowed by God Himself. They were not just the ordinary uncertainties of life.

The things that happened in the Book of Job are some of the mysteries of the Holy Bible. There was a scene in Heaven where Satan was present. God asked him where he had been. He responded that he had been to and fro in the Earth. Then the Lord asked him another question: *"Have you noticed my servant, Job, that there is none like him in all the Earth, a*

---

[15] Matthew Henry Commentary on Job
[16] Job 1:1

blameless and an upright man, one who fears God, and avoids evil?"

Satan raised objections against the compliments. As far as he was concerned, there was something that was the driving force behind Job's behavior. Job was only doing those things because he had been blessed so much. To prove his point, Satan challenged God to take away Job's blessings. This was the basis for all the unfortunate things that Job and his family experienced. But they didn't know what was going on. They had no idea why all these terrible things were happening to them.

Job was tested, and he passed the test with flying colors. He was a pioneer in his faith. He had no examples before him. He was one of the first to face such a difficult test. He had no one before him from whom to draw inspiration as to how to respond.

Even though he lost everything, Job did not turn his back on his God as Satan predicted. He proved Satan wrong. He did not serve God because of what God gave him, but because of who God is. Job trusted his God all the way, though he did not understand what was going on.

At the end of the story, God came on the scene. He confronted Job with a series of questions. He did not explain anything to Job. He did not owe Job any explanation or apology. It was Job who had to apologize before God. After this encounter, God blessed Job double in whatever he had. The exception was the children. He gave back the ten children Job lost.

What inspiration can we draw from this story? We must never give up on God no matter what life may bring our way. From Job's story, we discover that the righteous can face difficult times in life. People do not necessarily face hardships in life because of the sins they have committed. That was the conclusion of Job's friends. We must never be quick to give interpretation to a situation of life in the lives of others. Only God knows the 'whys' of life. It is important to understand and accept that God does not owe us an explanation for what life may bring our way. Trusting in Him means trusting Him to work out things for our good and His glory.

Daniel

Nothing negative is revealed about the character of Daniel. The same thing is true about Joseph, the son of Jacob. This does not suggest that they were perfect. It simply means that the Scripture is silent on the negative side of their lives. An extensive amount of information is revealed about both men, but nothing negative is said.

Daniel was one of the young men who were carried away into captivity in Babylon. Though far away from home and family, yet Daniel remained faithful to His God. He was one of the pioneers in the faith. His unshakable faith in the true living God has inspired the faith of so many people who know his story.

Daniel and all the faith pioneers became great people by their association with the great God. Daniel was a man of prayer. He prayed in good times and bad times. Prayer was just part of his life. A major challenge in his life was related to his prayer lifestyle. He refused to pray to another god, but only the true living God of Israel. As a result of this, he was thrown into a den of lions as punishment. But his God was there with him. He prevented the lions from hurting Daniel. His deliverance is one of the most interesting and dramatic stories in the Holy Bible.

Daniel's story has been one of inspiration to those who believe in Israel's true living God. The God of Daniel exists, and He is very real. He is like none other. He is in a class by Himself. Those who trust in Him will not be disappointed. It is this conviction that drives them to obey God no matter what the cost may be.

Daniel lived up to the common saying that *"No man is an island."* He was not a "one-man army" type of person. He bonded with others who believed as he did. He had Shadrach, Meshack, and Abednego as companions. Together, they were able to plead before God to deliver them from the decree of King Nebuchadnezzar. There is the need for believers to bond together as they live and hope in their God. In unity, there is strength. It is God's will that we are united in heart and our mission in this world.

The Apostle Paul

Time cannot permit us to continue. However, we cannot end without mentioning another character from the New Testament. Among the many that could have been chosen, I have selected the Apostle Paul and Timothy to represent the rest.

If you were to survey favorite characters from the New Testament, Paul's name would be among those at the top. Who was Paul? Like some characters in the Bible, his name was changed. His name was changed from Saul to Paul. Abraham, Sarah, and Jacob had their name changed.

Before his conversion, Paul was a very devoted Pharisee. He was born in the city of Tarsus, Cilicia. He was Gamaliel's student, a well-respected rabbi of the first century, an expert on Jewish laws.

The Pharisees were one of the religious groups during the time of Jesus Christ. They were the conservative group of their time. They believed in life after death. This was one of Paul's most profound convictions. Unlike the Sadducees, the Pharisees believed in the resurrection of the dead.

Paul's life serves as a classic example of the possibility of an individual being religious and yet not be saved. He was a religious Jew but ignorant of the salvation that God has ordained through Jesus Christ. Other examples are Lydia and Cornelius. We shall talk about them later.

This is a truth that some people find very difficult to process and accept. But according to God's program, everlasting life is found only in Jesus Christ. God ordains him to be the Savior of the world. He alone tasted death for all people.

The Biblical account is very clear. The Book of Acts says that there is no other name through which salvation can be obtained, apart from the name of Jesus Christ.[17] Jesus Himself said the same thing. *"Jesus said unto him, I am the way, the truth, and the life: no man comes unto the Father, but by Me."*[18]

After his encounter with Jesus on the road to Damascus, Paul realized that though he was religious, he was not saved. This realization must have come as a shock to him, who thought he was doing God's will. He made mention of this in his writings.[19]

A lady named Lydia and a man called Cornelius were also religious but needed to be saved through Jesus Christ. Lydia's story is found in the Book of Acts (chapter 16). She lived in the city of Philippi. She was a worshipper of God. She was either a Jew or one who had been converted to the Jewish religion. Apparently, whatever light that God had given to Lydia, she responded to that light. This must have been the reason why greater light was given to her.

During Paul's missionary journey, he and his team stopped in the city of Philippi. As was their usual practice, they went out for service on the Sabbath Day. The service was held on the bank of a river. Among the attendees was Lydia. As Paul preached, we are told that God opened Lydia's heart, and she believed. She believed in the salvation through Jesus Christ that Paul preached.

Cornelius's story is also found in the Book of Acts (chapter 10). Like Lydia, he was a worshipper of God. He was a devout, God-fearing man. He and his entire household were followers

---

17 Acts 4:12
18 John 14:6
19 Philippians 3:4-9; I Timothy 1:12-16

of God. He was sensitive to the needs of others and went out of his way to meet those needs. In addition to all this, Cornelius was a man of prayer. Whatever light God gave Cornelius, he responded in the right way. And as in Lydia's case, God gave him more light that led to his true conversion. God sent His servant, Peter, to Cornelius's house to preach the gospel of Jesus Christ to him and his family. At first, Peter hesitated to go to the house of a Gentile, but after a dramatic vision and a special delegation sent to him, Peter agreed to go. Upon his arrival, Peter asked Cornelius why he had sent for him. Cornelius told him that God had instructed him to send for him to preach God's word to them.

Following Cornelius's explanation, Peter made a profound statement: *"Then Peter opened his mouth and said, of a truth, I perceive that God is no respecter of persons: but in every nation, he that fears God and works righteousness, is accepted with Him."*[20]

As Peter preached the Word of God to Cornelius and his family, the Holy Spirit of God fell on all who were sitting under the sound of his voice. The salvation of God, ordained through Jesus Christ, was given to Cornelius and his family.

The examples of Paul, Lydia, and Cornelius indicate that God in His mercy and grace gives more light to those who respond to the light given them. Each of them had some knowledge about God, but the everlasting life that God provides through Jesus Christ was absent in them. It is this eternal life that qualifies an individual to enter into Heaven. This life is in Jesus Christ; He is everlasting life. All those who know Him as Savior have eternal life. Anyone who doesn't know Him does not have everlasting life. It is just that simple. This is an

---

20 Acts 10:34-35

objective revelation from God Himself. This is why the Great Commission that Jesus gave to His disciples is absolutely necessary. The gospel of Jesus Christ must be preached in all the world. It is a universal message designed to meet a universal need. That need is deliverance from the penalty of sin, which is hell.

Paul's life reveals important facts about the character of God and Paul's own character. The Bible tells us that God is gracious, merciful, longsuffering, and not willing that any should perish. That disposition of God is seen on display in Paul's life. The Lord was merciful to him. God was good to Paul. He did not get what he deserved. Out of ignorance, he followed and served God. Because of that, Paul could not see all that God was doing in the world. When Jesus came, Paul did not know that His coming was part of God's plan. That is why he opposed Jesus and His ministry. Little did he know that in his zeal, he was opposing and fighting against God. But the Lord had mercy on Paul. He went out of His way to save him in a very dramatic way.

A preacher once said that if anyone deserved to end up in hell, it was Paul. But it was not God's will for Paul to end up in hell. God is not interested in the death of the wicked. It took God Himself to bring Paul to his knees. That is why he was so grateful to the Lord for his salvation.

God's incredible display of His mercy affected Paul's character. He was never the same again. After meeting Jesus, he stopped persecuting and killing Christians; he was now one of them. He was totally broken. He surrendered his life to Jesus. His life was characterized by gratitude and appreciation to God. It was this frame of mind that shaped his devotion and involvement in ministry. He was committed to doing everything in his power to get God's work done. His attitude must have affected those who worked along with him. Timothy and the other men associated with Paul were also devoted to the Lord's work. Salvation can change our attitude and behavior.

PART THREE

SPECIAL EXAMPLE OF INSPIRATION

Inspired By God Himself

The Lord God is the greatest motivator. We can learn so much from each person of the Godhead. God is one, but He exists as three in one: Father, Son, and Holy Spirit. They all interact with mankind.

From God the Father, we see the greatest display of love for mankind. It was His love that moved Him to send His Son to die in our place as a sacrificial Lamb for the sin of the world. His love prevented Him from sparing His Son. He allowed Him to die a cruel death on our behalf. He loved the world so much that He gave His only begotten Son. God is love. Love is part of His nature. That love is simply defined as *"one seeking the very best for another."* God's love is not dependent on who we are and how we behave. The Bible tells us that He displayed His love for us when we were sinners and enemies of God.[21]

God is our example of love. We are commanded and challenged to love one another. We are to love other human beings, irrespective of who they are and how they behave. Believers are to seek the very best for other people, regardless of their race, national identity, and social status.

God is presented in the Bible as being merciful, gracious, longsuffering, and abundant in goodness and truth.[22] According to Jonah's testimony, God is also slow to get angry

---

21 Romans 5:8
22 Exodus 33:6

and willing to forgive.[23] That is God's character. We are commanded to imitate Him.[24]

In our dealings with other people, we are to show mercy, be good, be patient, and be people of truth. We must put off all falsehood, for there is no falsehood with God.

There is so much we can learn from God the Son. He was obedient unto the Father and cooperated with the Father in all things. Just as Isaac cooperated with his father to do God's will, Jesus did the same thing.

Jesus was a man of love. It was His love for humanity that He became our sacrificial Lamb. He made that clear to His disciples: *"Greater love has no man than this, that a man lays down His life for His friends."*[25] Jesus' love is great. It has no comparison among the children of men. He was the greatest friend who ever lived. He sought the very best for His friends.

Jesus desires that as many as possible may enter into the kingdom of God. He died to make that possible. Through His death, He placed the world in a savable position. Those who want to be saved can be saved. He will not reject anyone who comes to Him.

Jesus lived His life on Earth in such a way that demonstrated He wants people to go to Heaven. He went from village to village, town to town, preaching the Word of God. He encouraged people to believe and be saved. Before He went back to Heaven, He commanded His disciples to go into all the world to preach the gospel to all people.

If He wants people to be saved and enter into Heaven, that should be all His followers' desire. We should not only desire

---

23 Jonah 4:2
24 Ephesians 5:1
25 John 15:13

people to be saved; we should show it by telling them about the Good News.

The third person of the Godhead is the Holy Spirit. He is the one who convicts us of sin and reveals our need for a Savior. When we believe the gospel of Jesus Christ, He seals us and places us in the family of God. He is the one who inspires and empowers us to worship and serve God.

With all this going for us, believers in Jesus Christ have all the reasons to rejoice and be glad in the Lord in this world. Indeed, we are more than conquerors through Him who saved us and gave us a reason to live.

CONCLUSION

Inspiration is the urge that motivates us to push ahead or initial a new path. It energizes us to take action that can benefit us as well as other people. As it relates to our faith, through others' faith, we, too, have been inspired to trust God more and always. When we are inspired, we expect great things from God and attempt great things for His honor and glory.

We have an advantage because we are not pioneers in the faith. Others have paved the path to follow. We can learn from their good decisions. Those decisions can help to shape how we respond to the challenges of life. If God could do it for them, He can also do it for us when we trust in Him.

NOTES

1 Jeremiah 17:9
2 Hebrews 11:17-19
3 Genesis 15:6
4 Acts 17:11
5 James 1:17
6 I Corinthians 4:7
7 Psalm 55:22
8 Matthew 10:8
9 Mark 16:15
10 Proverbs 16:17
11 Genesis 6:5
12 Hebrews 11:7
13 II Peter 3
14 John 3:14-17
15 Matthew Henry Commentary on Job
16 Job 1:1
17 Acts 4:12
18 John 14:6
19 Philippians 3:4-9; I Timothy 1:12-16
20 Acts 10:34-35
21 Romans 5:8
22 Exodus 33:6
23 Jonah 4:2
24 Ephesians 5:1
25 John 15:13

BIBLIOGRAPHY

Holy Bible. Nashville: Thomas Nelson, 1989.

Matthew Henry. "Commentary on Job." Christianity Today.com, 2021.

Quao, Arikana Chihombori. Africa 101: The Wake Up Call, Foxworth Consulting LCC, 2020.

Wallace, Carey. "White American Christianity Needs to be Honest About Its History of White Supremacy."

Pastor and Mrs Whiangar

The Whiangar's children: Tenizi, Tehmen, Tuakah, and Tamayn.

Available on Amazon and where books are sold.

Pub Date: July 17, 2019
Format: Paperback
Pages: 142
ISBN-10 : 1945408456
ISBN-13 : 978-1945408458
Size: 5.5 x 8.5 inches

An amazing story of love and grace.

"*He Has Included Us recounts the story of how a very poor boy living in Liberia comes to faith in Christ and experiences a complete transformation of his life in every way. As you read Tuakah's story, you will no doubt be able to sense God's love for him, but even more, you will also begin to sense God's amazing love for you.*"

Bishop Darlington Johnson, General Overseer, Bethel World

www.ingramcontent.com/pod-product-compliance
Lightning Source LLC
Chambersburg PA
CBHW052124110526
44592CB00013B/1736